WEATHER SAFETY

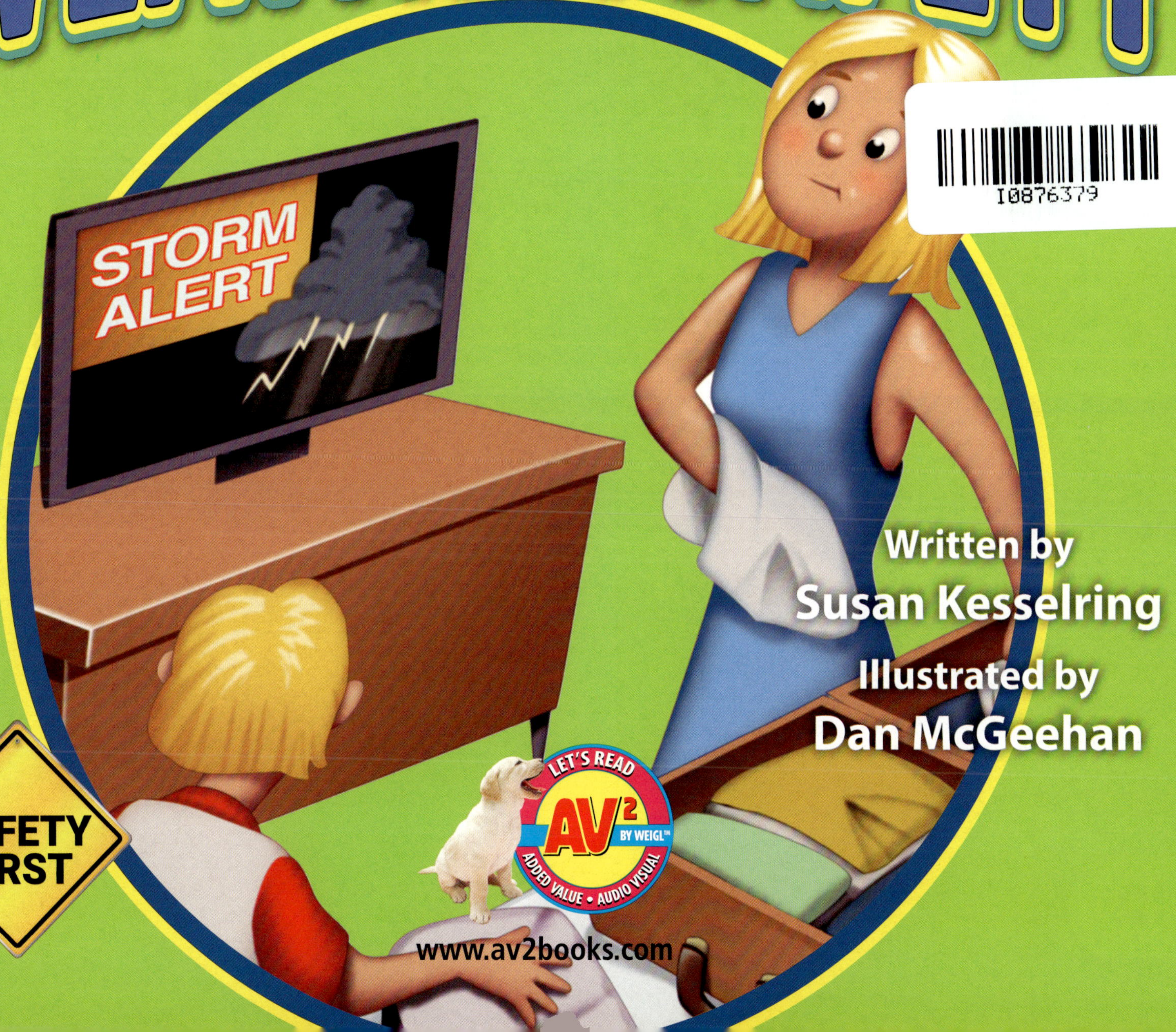

Written by
Susan Kesselring
Illustrated by
Dan McGeehan

SAFETY FIRST

www.av2books.com

Published by AV^2 by Weigl
350 5th Avenue, 59th Floor New York, NY 10118
Website: www.av2books.com

Library of Congress Cataloging-in-Publication Data

Names: Kesselring, Susan, author.
Title: Weather safety / Susan Kesselring.
Other titles: Being safe with weather
Description: New York, NY : AV^2 by Weigl, [2019] | Series: Safety first | Audience: K to Grade 3. |
Identifiers: LCCN 2018053401 (print) | LCCN 2018054321 (ebook) | ISBN 9781489699817 (Multi User Ebook) | ISBN 9781489699824 (Single User Ebook) | ISBN 9781489699794 (hardcover : alk. paper) | ISBN 9781489699800 (softcover : alk. paper)
Subjects: LCSH: Storms--Juvenile literature. | Weather protection--Juvenile literature. | Weather--Physiological effect--Juvenile literature.
Classification: LCC QC941.3 (ebook) | LCC QC941.3 .K47 2019 (print) | DDC 363.34/92--dc23
LC record available at https://lccn.loc.gov/2018053401

Printed in the United States of America in Brainerd, Minnesota
1 2 3 4 5 6 7 8 9 0 22 21 20 19 18

112018
102918

Project Coordinator: Jared Siemens Designer: Ana María Vidal

First published by The Child's World in 2011

WEATHER SAFETY

In this book, you will learn about

weather safety,

what to do,

what not to do,

and much more!

What do you do in different kinds of weather? Do you splash in rain puddles or tumble in the snow? On a hot afternoon, do you eat a cold ice cream cone?

You can enjoy nature's weather, rain or shine. Just remember to follow some rules and you'll stay safe.

Rain waters plants and fills rivers, lakes, and streams. But too much rain can cause floods. A river's water can spill over onto the land around it.

If heavy rain is falling, check the news on the radio or television. There could be a flood warning. If a flood is near your home, go to higher ground. Do not try to wade or swim in floodwater. It could be very deep. It could be moving faster than you think, too.

Sometimes thunder and lightning come along with rain. It's a thunderstorm!

A thunderstorm is amazing to see. It has bright flashes and loud cracks. But always watch it from inside a building. If lightning strikes the building, you will still be safe.

Lightning can come inside through the wires of electronics. Don't use a phone with a cord or touch your television during a thunderstorm.

Bring a flashlight and a radio with batteries to the basement with you. Grab a game, too. You can play it while you wait for the storm to end.

A thunderstorm that brings large hail and strong winds is a severe thunderstorm. It could even include a tornado. This type of weather can damage buildings and homes.

In a severe thunderstorm or tornado, take cover. Go to the lowest level of your home to wait it out. Make sure you stay away from windows.

STORM
ALERT

Near the ocean, you might see a kind of storm called a hurricane. When a hurricane reaches land, its winds can blow over trees and signs. Hurricane winds move faster than a car moves on a highway. You should stay inside a building during a hurricane.

The ocean at the shore can rise about 20 feet (6 meters) during a hurricane. If this happens, you may have to leave your home until it passes.

Do you like to build snowmen in the snow? Make sure you stay warm and cozy. Bundle up with a jacket, snow pants, a scarf, mittens, and boots. Don't forget a hat! Wearing these things will keep you from getting frostbite.

When you begin to shiver or feel very tired, it's time for you to go inside and warm up.

It's fun to go sledding! But remember to play safely. Don't sled on ice or near roads. Have a parent watch you, too.

A blizzard usually means school is closed for the day. The blowing snow makes it hard to see even a few feet in front of you. Be sure to ask an adult first if it's safe to play outside.

It's easy to get lost outside during a blizzard. Winds blow at speeds more than 35 miles (56 kilometers) per hour. That's faster than your parents drive the family car through town.

STOP

What about when the weather turns muggy and hot? Do you ride a bike and play tag? It's fun to play outside in summer, but remember a few rules.

Drink lots of cold liquids. Wear clothing that keeps you cool, such as shorts and tank tops. Also, stay in the shade as much as you can.

Swimming in a pool or a lake is a great way to cool off. Always make sure there is an adult to watch you swim.

QUIET

Some days it is just too hot! You could get very sick if you ran around outside.

Stay inside your home and keep the air conditioning on. If your home does not have air conditioning, spend some time at a cool library reading a book.

TODAY
SUNNY
TOMORROW
RAIN

Remember to always keep an eye to the sky. Check out the weather report to learn what weather is headed your way. That will keep you safe, both indoors and out!

KEY WORDS

Research has shown that as much as 65 percent of all written material published in English is made up of 300 words. These 300 words cannot be taught using pictures or learned by sounding them out. They must be recognized by sight. This book contains 119 common sight words to help young readers improve their reading fluency and comprehension. This book also teaches young readers several important content words, such as proper nouns.

Page	Sight Words First Appearance
4	a, different, do, eat, in, kinds, of, on, or, the, what, you
5	and, be, can, follow, for, have, how, I, just, me, some, tell, to, watch, will, with
7	around, but, could, go, home, if, is, it, land, much, near, news, not, over, plants, rivers, than, there, think, too, try, very, waters, your
9	along, always, come, don't, from, has, it's, see, sometimes, still, through, use
10	end, play, while
11	away, even, large, make, out, take, that, this
13	about, at, car, feet, its, leave, may, might, move, should, trees, until, when
15	keep, like, these, things, time, up
17	an, ask, day, family, few, first, get, hard, means, miles, more, school
19	also, as, great, off, such, turns, way
21	air, book, does
23	both, eye, learn

Page	Content Words First Appearance
4	afternoon, ice cream cone, rain puddles, snow, weather
5	nature, rain, rules, shine
7	floods, higher ground, lakes, radio, streams, television
9	building, cord, cracks, electronics, flashes, lightning, phone, thunder, thunderstorm, wires
10	basement, batteries, flashlight, game, radio, storm
11	hail, tornado, windows, winds
13	highway, hurricane, ocean, shore, signs
15	boots, frostbite, hat, ice, jacket, mittens, roads, scarf, snow pants, parent, snowmen
17	adult, blizzard, outside, town
19	bike, clothing, liquids, pool, shade, shorts, summer, tag, tank tops
21	air conditioning, library
23	indoors, sky, weather report